RHYMING ON RUSHMORE

FROM A TO Z

RHYMING ON RUSHMORE

FROM A TO Z

By Jodi Holley Latza
Modern Photography by Greg Latza

Published by the Mount Rushmore History Association

MOUNT RUSHMORE

HISTORY ASSOCIATION

Supporting Education at Mount Rushmore Since 1993

Published by the Mount Rushmore History Association
Written by Jodi Holley Latza
Photography (unless otherwise noted) by Greg Latza
Art Direction & Design: Julie Sullivan Design, Flagstaff, Arizona
Editors: Education Specialist Rhonda Buell Schier and Debbie Ketel
Copy Editor: Mary Anne Maier
Project Manager: Debbie Ketel
Reviewed by Chief of Interpretation Judy Olson
Printed in Canada

Library of Congress Cataloging-in-Publication Data
Latza, Jodi Holley.
Rhyming on Rushmore : from A-Z / by Jodi Latza.
     p. cm.
ISBN 0-9752617-5-4 (alk. paper)
1. Mount Rushmore National Memorial (S.D.)--Juvenile literature.
2. English language--Alphabet--Juvenile literature. I. Title.
 F657.R8L38 2005
 978.3'93--dc22

              2005003071

Mount Rushmore History Association
www.mtrushmorebookstore.com
13000 Hwy 244 . Bldg 31 . Suite 2
Keystone, SD 57751 . 1-800-699-3142

As a committee of the Mount Rushmore National Memorial Society, the Mount Rushmore History Association's mission is to support and assist the National Park Service with educational, historical, and interpretive activities at Mount Rushmore National Memorial.

Dedication

For Jack, who soon will be learning his ABCs,
and Luke and Anna, who will be doing their best to help him

A IS FOR AMERICA

Mount Rushmore embodies
the hopeful foundation
Of an independent, fair,
democratic nation.
A home for all people,
despite wealth or needs,
AMERICA welcomes
all colors and creeds.

Did you know? Mount Rushmore represents 150 years of American history and the birth, growth, preservation and development of the United States of America.

Sculptor at hand,
true patriot at heart,
Gutzon **BORGLUM**
carved stone into breathtaking art.
With passion, persistence
and strong Danish pride,
His talent transformed
a whole mountainside.

B

IS FOR BORGLUM

Did you know? Gutzon Borglum was born in Idaho in 1867. He was a talented artist who had experience carving mountains at a place called Stone Mountain, Georgia. South Dakota State Historian Doane Robinson had the idea to carve a mountain in the Black Hills and invited Borglum to visit South Dakota in 1924. The rest is history!

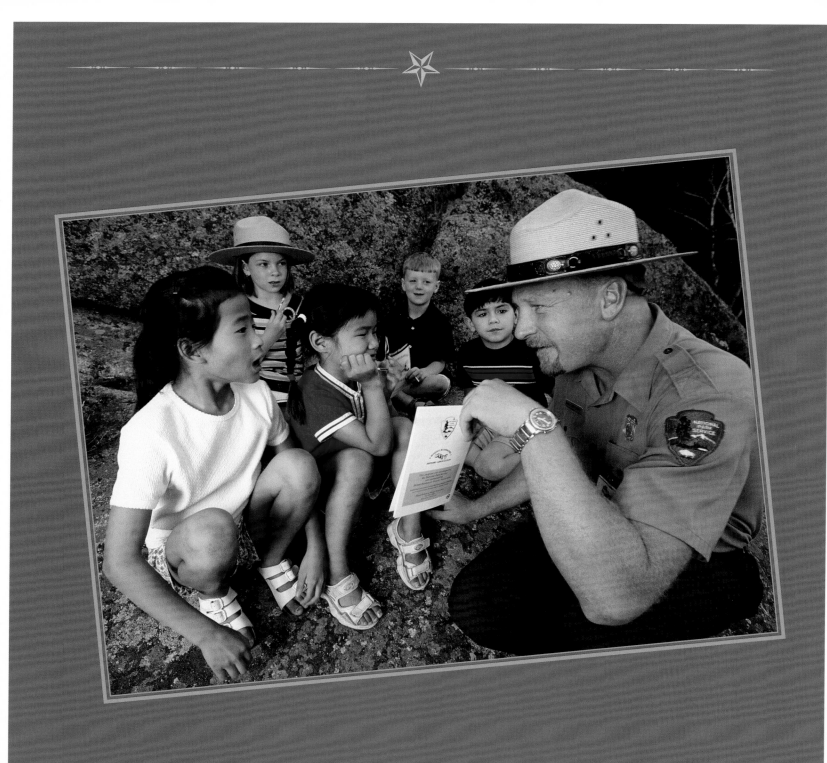

IS FOR CHILDREN

CHILDREN will find
lots of things that they like:
There are animals, ice cream
and places to hike.
Go exploring with
the Junior Ranger crew
For many more fun things
to see and to do!

 Did you know? Children ages 5 through
12 can participate in the Mount Rushmore
Junior Ranger program in which they learn how
and why the mountain was carved.

D IS FOR DYNAMITE

Detonating **DYNAMITE** and drilling
Are what make carving a mountain so thrilling!
When Borglum was blasting, great booms filled the air,
Giving people and wildlife nearby quite a scare.

Did you know? Dynamite blasted away 900 million pounds of rock to reach stone that could be carved.

Using light and shadow,
form and scale,
The **EYES** of Mount Rushmore
reveal a tale
Of American vision,
courage and drive,
Helping the sculpture
to come alive.

IS FOR EYES

Did you know? Borglum told the carvers to leave a 20-inch shaft of granite in the center of each eye. The ends of these shafts reflect the sunlight, make the eyes sparkle and bring the presidents to life.

IS FOR FLAGS

Unfurled at the foot
of the four great faces
Is a welcome to folks
from faraway places.
Fifty-six **FLAGS**
flying proudly and free,
As symbols of goodwill
and unity.

Did you know? The flags of all the states,
districts, territories and commonwealths of the
USA are displayed on Mount Rushmore's
Avenue of Flags. Guam, American Samoa and
the Virgin Islands are American territories.
Puerto Rico and the Northern Mariana Islands
are commonwealths, and, then there is the
District of Columbia.

G IS FOR GRANITE

Rock in the Black Hills
called Harney Peak **GRANITE**
Is some of the oldest stone
found on the planet.
Hard and long-lasting,
it's solid and dense.
To use it for carving
just seems to make sense.

Did you know? Harney Peak granite is found only in the Black Hills of South Dakota!

H IS FOR HALL OF RECORDS

Ten thousand years from now,
people will know
How our forefathers spelled it out,
so long ago.
The **HALL OF RECORDS**
will still hold the key,
Explaining our commitment
to liberty.

☞ **Did you know?** The Hall of Records contains important documents from American history, including the Constitution and Declaration of Independence, which are replicated on 2-by-4-foot porcelain enamel panels. These panels are housed in an underground vault located in a canyon opposite the back of the Mount Rushmore sculpture.

I IS FOR INDEPENDENCE DAY

INDEPENDENCE DAY
serves as a grand celebration,
A huge birthday party
for our beloved nation.
Fireworks light up
the summertime sky
One special evening,
each and every July.

Did you know? One of the biggest fireworks displays in the country is held at Mount Rushmore each July 3rd. The Independence Day celebration is packed full of patriotic events such as military band concerts, aircraft fly-overs and a flag-folding ceremony.

J

IS FOR JEFFERSON

Thomas **JEFFERSON**
declared America free,
Sent Lewis and Clark west
to find the sea
And made the greatest
land purchase in history,
Expanding our borders
significantly.

Did you know? In 1803, Jefferson, our third president, negotiated America's purchase of the 828,000-square-mile Louisiana Territory from France for $15 million, almost doubling the size of the United States.

Sure-footed babies,
white fuzzballs in action,
Mountain goat **KIDS**
are a springtime attraction.
Since 1924,
they've roamed the Black Hills,
Impressing visitors
with their rock-hopping skills.

IS FOR KIDS

 Did you know? Mountain goats are great climbers due to their long, split hooves. The bottoms of their hooves have soft pads that cling to the rocks.

L IS FOR LINCOLN

Commonly known
by his famous nickname,
"Abe" **LINCOLN**
wanted everyone treated the same.
He preserved the union
and helped set the slaves free
When the North and the South
simply could not agree.

Did you know? Abraham Lincoln, the
16th American president, was a gifted speaker
who delivered one of the most famous
speeches in history, his 1863 address at the
Civil War battlefield at Gettysburg, Pennsylvania.

M IS FOR MOUNTAIN

Majestic and solid,
a gem in the rough,
This **MOUNTAIN** was destined
for important stuff.
Named on a whim,
for a New York attorney
Who came to the Hills
on a prospecting journey.

Did you know? Mount Rushmore was named after Charles E. Rushmore, a lawyer who visited the Black Hills several times on business in 1884 and 1885. As the story goes, the local miners took a liking to Rushmore, naming the mountain for him after he asked whether it had a name.

Since before these four leaders
were widely renowned,
NATIVE AMERICANS
have lived on this sacred ground.
As they share their traditions,
stories and art,
We can learn of their culture
and all play a part.

IS FOR NATIVE AMERICANS

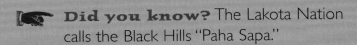 **Did you know?** The Lakota Nation
calls the Black Hills "Paha Sapa."

IS FOR OCTOBER

For fourteen long years,
days and weeks came and went.
As the months slipped away,
time was borrowed and spent.
OCTOBER brings frost
and the splendor of fall
And marks the beginning
and end of it all.

 Did you know? Carving on Mount Rushmore began October 4, 1927, and ended October 31, 1941.

P IS FOR PRESIDENTIAL TRAIL

Take the **PRESIDENTIAL TRAIL**
along the forest floor
To get as close as you can
to the fabulous four.
Smell the pine-scented air
and enjoy the cool breeze,
Then drink in the view
for as long as you please.

👉 **Did you know?** The Presidential Trail gives visitors a close-up view of the faces. The trail winds a half mile through fragrant ponderosa pines, the trees that make the Black Hills appear black from a distance.

Scattered into granite
as white crystals in stone,
QUARTZ has a beauty
uniquely its own.
It sparkles and glistens
and catches the eye,
Like sunbeams embracing
this mountain so high.

IS FOR QUARTZ

Did you know? The minerals quartz, feldspar and mica make up the granite texture of Mount Rushmore.

R IS FOR ROOSEVELT

ROOSEVELT lived
for strenuous chores.
As a horseman and hunter,
he loved the outdoors.
He developed our country
by setting in motion
The plan for a shortcut
between the two oceans.

Did you know? During his two terms as the 26th president, Theodore Roosevelt helped develop the United States by initiating the construction of the Panama Canal as a shorter route between the East and West. He is also known for designating 5 national parks, 150 national forests and 18 national monuments.

S

IS FOR SCULPTOR'S STUDIO

Visit the **SCULPTOR'S STUDIO**
and find
The challenges met
by an artist's mind;
A place for measuring,
plotting and planning
With a window, convenient
for mountain scanning.

Did you know? The Sculptor's Studio is one of three that Gutzon Borglum used during the carving of Mount Rushmore. He first created a model of the four presidents and then used a "pointing system" to copy his art to the mountain. The studio still houses the original model.

IS FOR TOOLS

No normal hammer,
file, chisel or pick
Could carve into granite
so strong and so thick
As jackhammers, wedges
and dynamite:
The perfect **TOOLS** needed
to sculpt it just right.

☛ **Did you know?** First, dynamite blasted rock. Then, workers used jackhammers to drill holes in the surface, a process called "honeycombing." Next, mallets and wedges were used to pry off stone left between the holes. In the final stage of carving, called "bumping," a special four-star bit was used to finish the sculpture's surface, making it smooth as a sidewalk.

U
IS FOR UPHILL

Seven hundred and sixty steps up to the top,
Carvers climbed in all weather, rarely calling a stop
To this labor of love, with its struggle **UPHILL**,
Which demanded sheer guts and a powerful will.

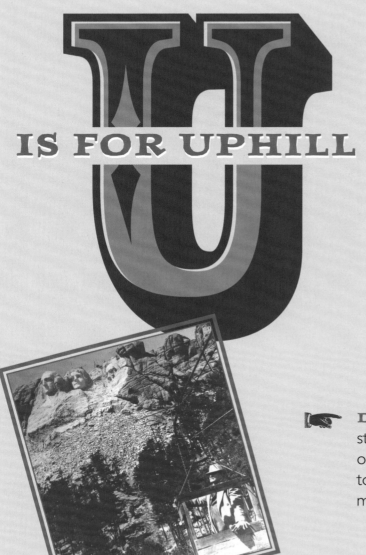

Did you know? Aside from climbing the steps, there was one other way to reach the top of Mount Rushmore. An aerial tramway carried tools, supplies and people from the base of the mountain to the top of Roosevelt's head.

IS FOR VISITORS

Nearly three million **VISITORS**
gather each year
On the Grand View Terrace
and areas near,
In the heart of our nation,
the Land of the Free,
Where we value the spirit
of democracy.

Did you know? A democracy is
a form of government in which every
citizen has a vote.

A farmer turned soldier,
George **WASHINGTON** fought
For the free, happy homeland
all colonists sought.
He defeated the British,
a historic event
That made him the choice
for our first president.

Did you know? George Washington was one of two presidents to sign the Constitution. (The other was fourth president James Madison.) He was also the only U.S. president in history to receive all of the votes cast by the electoral college.

IS FOR WASHINGTON

MARKS THE SPOT

X MARKS THE SPOT
where a sculptor once stood
And sized up this mountain,
calling it good.
It had natural majesty
in every way
And was bathed in the sunlight
for most of the day.

 Did you know? Gutzon Borglum picked
Mount Rushmore because its southeast exposure
provided the proper lighting and the granite mass
was large enough to accommodate the planned
sculpture.

Y

IS FOR YOU

Long ago, when this nation was just starting out, People were learning what freedom was about. They looked to the future, with hopes high and true And built a great country for me and for **YOU**.

Did you know? Some new Americans take their oath of citizenship before the Shrine of Democracy as they adopt America as their home and pledge to live as good citizens.

Z IS FOR ZEAL

Borglum was one
who believed he could do
Nearly any task
that he would set his mind to.
His tenacity, foresight
and uncommon **ZEAL**
Helped bring this site
monumental appeal.

☞ **Did you know?** Gutzon Borglum is an example for any of us who face a big challenge. He was known for saying: "Don't say 'I can't' on this work. The 'I can'ts' are unknown in the world's work and unremembered in history."

Photo Credits

All photographs are by Greg Latza unless noted below.

p. 5   Background photo by Rise Studio
p. 8   Background photo by Rise Studio
p. 9   Color photo from Lincoln Borglum Collection
          Bottom photo by Bell Photo
p. 10   Lincoln Borglum Collection
p. 13   Background photo by Manugian Studios, Stamford, CT, Charles d'Emery
p. 16   Background photo by Bell Photo
          Inset photo courtesy of the White House Historical Association
p. 18   Courtesy of the White House Historical Association
p. 19   Publisher's Photo Service
p. 20   Background photo by Rise Studio
          Inset photo courtesy of the National Park Service
p. 23   Rise Studio
p. 26   Bell Photo
p. 27   Courtesy of the White House Historical Association
p. 30   Rise Studio
p. 33   Background photo by Bell Photo
          Inset photo courtesy of the White House Historical Association
p. 37   Background photo by Charles d'Emery